MW01047280

THE PRINCIPLES

OF

DELIVERANCE

Apostle Dr. Glen A. England

© Copyright All Rights Reserved. Joshua Ministries Int'l. Principles Of
Deliverance

DEDICATION

My first book is dedicated to my beautiful wide, Prophetess Karen England, who has stood with me through the various seasons of my life since our youth. Her love, prayer and submission have helped me become what God has made me to be.

My eternal love is to God, who gave her to me, not only as my wife, but also as the mother of my four beautiful children. May God bless her greatly and cause the apostolic and prophetic dimension in her life to be perfected.

© Copyright All Rights Reserved. Joshua Ministries Int'l. Principles Of Deliverance

© Copyright All Rights Reserved. Joshua Ministries Int'l. Principles Of Deliverance

MANY THANKS TO....

Our Lord and Savior Jesus Christ, Who called and commissioned me to be an apostle of deliverance, and an ambassadorial apostle to the nations.

My wife Karen, and my children, Shianne (for conducting research and typing) and Shalisha, Kelvin and Glenville, his wife, Kesha. And also my spiritual daughter, Chelsea (for her assistance). Not forgetting my granddaughter, Amazing England.

Apostle James Duncan and his wife, Prophetess Donna Duncan, for providing spiritual covering over me.

Valencia Lindsay, who also assisted with this book.

All of my Joshua Ministries International family for their prayers and support.

Harrison Forde for cover design and general assistance.

5
© Copyright All Rights Reserved. Joshua Ministries Int'l. Principles Of Deliverance

Acknowledgements

My greatest thank you must first be expressed to the Lord

for the grace He placed upon me to write this book.

Through the leading of the Holy Spirit He has equipped me

with the knowledge and understanding of the spiritual

world. He has commissioned me to go out and share that

same knowledge to the world to build up warriors in the

body of Christ and tear down every ancient and religious

beliefs. I extend heartfelt thanks to my beautiful wife

Prophetess Karen England who has been a true help mate

and has supported, encouraged and pushed the birthing of

this book and my life as an Apostle and deliverance

minister. To my lovely children who have also shared in

this dream and even put their hands to the plough to ensure

this book came into being, thanks.

6
© Copyright All Rights Reserved. Joshua Ministries Int'l. Principles Of
Deliverance

I must also thank my spiritual father and General Overseer Apostle Dr. James Duncan and his lovely wife, my spiritual mother, Prophetess Donna Duncan who has nurtured and, counseled me and prophecied God's heart for my life. They have and continue to be a great source of guidance and strength. To Apostle Gladstone Hazel, my spiritual granddad, I also express thanks for pushing me to write about deliverance and over the years offering wise counsel. To my late spiritual mother, Prophetess Muriel Weeks, who spoke the heart of God over my life many years ago and made sure I was placed in the right spiritual company before she died, I express sincere appreciation. Esteemed thanks to my biological father Glen A England Senior and my late mother Maureen England who loved me tirelessly and nurtured me the best they could, again thank you. To all my family members including my in-laws, I say thank you. I am grateful.

© Copyright All Rights Reserved. Joshua Ministries Int'l. Principles Of Deliverance

© Copyright All Rights Reserved. Joshua Ministries Int'l. Principles Of
Deliverance

Table of Contents

© Copyright All Rights Reserved. Joshua Ministries Int'l. Principles Of Deliverance

© Copyright All Rights Reserved. Joshua Ministries Int'l. Principles Of
Deliverance

Introduction

This book seeks to equip believers with the tools necessary

for the Ministry of Deliverance. It also serves to enlighten

the spiritual understanding of the church, bring clarity

about the true meaning of deliverance, and confirm the fact

that this is indeed the Ministry of Jesus Christ.

"Deliverance, is the action of being rescued or set free."

Jesus Christ Himself went about setting the captives free

from the bondage of Satan. Mark 16:15-18 (KJV) says,

And he said unto them, Go ye into all the world, and

preach the gospel to every creature. He that believeth and

is baptized shall be saved; but he that believeth not shall be

damned. And these signs shall follow them that believe; In

my name shall they cast out devils; they shall speak with

new tongues; They shall take up serpents; and if they drink

© Copyright All Rights Reserved. Joshua Ministries Int'l. Principles Of Deliverance

any deadly thing, it shall not hurt them; they shall lay

hands on the sick, and they shall recover.

Jesus made it clear in these verses that deliverance

and/or casting out devils, are some of the signs that a true

born-again believer should possess.

© Copyright All Rights Reserved. Joshua Ministries Int'l. Principles Of
Deliverance

The Given Power

The given power refers to the "God-given" permission, impartation or transfer of ability or authority to every born-again believer in Christ Jesus. As heirs of God, we have access to this given power to dismantle Satan's kingdom. Without such power you have no protective legal grounds to come against or destroy the kingdom of darkness.

As indicated in Luke 10:19 KJV, *Behold, I give unto you power to tread on serpents and scorpions, and over all the power of the enemy: and nothing shall by any means hurt you.* This scripture is a direct representation of the power given to us as sons of God to destroy Satan's kingdom and the assurance of protection once we activate such power as the verse says: *and nothing shall by any means hurt you*

—"the believer and possessor of power"

13

© Copyright All Rights Reserved. Joshua Ministries Int'l. Principles Of Deliverance

To achieve deliverance we must first understand the authority we have as children of the Kingdom and what we have authority and power over.

Luke 10:19 also specifies who gave us power (God) and what we have power over.

This includes the power to:

1. Tread upon (to trample, to put under foot, to take away power) serpents and scorpions (symbols of demonic spirits)

2. Overcome the power of the enemy (principalities and powers)

To further explain,   the Greek word for power is "dunamis" which means:

- strength, power and ability

- inherent power, power residing in a thing by virtue of its nature, or which a person or thing exerts or puts forth

14
© Copyright All Rights Reserved. Joshua Ministries Int'l. Principles Of Deliverance

- delegated authority granted to a person or persons in a particular office

- power for performing miracles

- moral power and excellence of soul

- the power and influence which belongs to riches and wealth

- power and resources arising from others

- power consisting in or resting upon armies, force, host

God gave the church (His body) the power to destroy Satan's kingdom. Therefore, the church must move from the avenue of religion to carry out its God-given responsibilities and trample Satan under its foot. God has released his power, and is waiting for his children to activate and establish it by faith.

It is spiritually legal to say that we, as born-again believers and children of the Kingdom, have been given power to render Satan's kingdom powerless. God is looking

15

© Copyright All Rights Reserved. Joshua Ministries Int'l. Principles Of Deliverance

for His authority and power to be demonstrated through us against the kingdom of darkness on a daily basis, through the undeniable Act of Deliverance and the Power of The Holy Ghost.

Romans 8:19 KJV *For the earnest expectation of the creature waiteth for the manifestation of the sons of God.* This scripture ensures us as children of God that all of creation is waiting on us to manifest our God-given power to bring liberty to them that are bound.

Therefore, as heirs of God, we must clearly understand and know that we were given the power over every satanic attack against our lives as well as authority to sever every demonic scheme. It must be in accordance with the HOLY GHOST. It is the Holy Ghost that performs the act of deliverance on our behalf. God gave us power as His children so that we can establish his Kingdom here on earth and demonstrate authority against the works of darkness. It brings awareness to Satan that God's children are in charge

© Copyright All Rights Reserved. Joshua Ministries Int'l. Principles Of Deliverance

once we activate and operate in our given power. This power is a direct activation of the Holy Spirit, which desires to dwell on the inside of all believers. Once you experience the baptism of the Holy Ghost, you experience a new level of power.

Luke 4:1 KJV *And Jesus being full of the Holy Ghost returned from Jordan, and was led by the Spirit into the wilderness.* Luke 4:14 KJV *And Jesus returned in the power of the Spirit into Galilee: and there went out a fame of him through all the region round about.* Jesus himself needed to be filled with God's power which came to Him by the Holy Spirit. Likewise, we only receive power when we accept the Holy Ghost.

Acts 1:8 (AMP) *But you will receive power and ability when the Holy Spirit comes upon you; and you will be My witnesses [to tell people about Me] both in Jerusalem and in all Judea, and Samaria, and even to the ends of the earth.*

© Copyright All Rights Reserved. Joshua Ministries Int'l. Principles Of Deliverance

Remember that the power comes when you receive the Holy Ghost. When the Holy Spirit comes upon you, you receive ability, efficiency and might to combat demonic interferences in your life. The Holy Ghost is like "kryptonite" to Satan and his co-host.

© Copyright All Rights Reserved. Joshua Ministries Int'l. Principles Of Deliverance

Principles of Deliverance

Deliverance is a method or act used by those who continue the ministry of Jesus to set the captive free here on Earth. Those who are bound by demons are being controlled by evil forces and the devil uses any and everything to gain control over a person's life. That person must undergo the process of deliverance in order to be set free.

The ministry of deliverance can be seen as a ministry of rescue or help for God's people. It helps God's people to break out of demonic prisons such as addictions, generational curses, ancestral curses and even self-imprisonment. These forms of imprisonments may come from seeking counsel from the works of witches or warlocks or those that practice devil worship and make sacrifices to the devil. Demonic altars may be erected in the life of those who engage in consultations with witch doctors or practice satanic sacrifices which in turn also

19

© Copyright All Rights Reserved. Joshua Ministries Int'l. Principles Of Deliverance

open doors for Satan and his co-host to have legal rights
and inhabit their lives.

- Deliverance also refers to: the action of being
  rescued or set free. It can be a formal or
  authoritative utterance; for example to direct, cast
  out, release, liberate or free from bondage.

Deliverance Formula:

This deliverance formula is based upon biblical and
spiritual principles to help a person receive the complete
and full benefits of deliverance. The first act of deliverance
is through salvation or accepting Jesus Christ as your
personal Lord and Saviour. This acceptance of Jesus Christ
breaks or dismisses Satan's legal rights to inhabit your life
and thereby enable you to surrender totally to Jesus Christ
for Him to take full control of your life. 1 John 5:12 (KJV)
*He that hath the Son hath life; and he that hath not the Son
of God hath not life.* The word of God declares that
deliverance is the "children's bread" in Matthew 15:26

© Copyright All Rights Reserved. Joshua Ministries Int'l. Principles Of
Deliverance

(KJV) *But he answered and said, It is not meet to take the children's bread, and to cast it to dogs.* This indicates that for deliverance to take place and be effective, there must be recognition and acceptance of Jesus Christ as Lord and Saviour. Without recognition and acceptance of Jesus Christ prior to deliverance, demons can still inhabit a person's life. Salvation is a critical step in the process of deliverance. Before we are cleansed, purged or delivered there must be confession of sins. 1 John 1: 9 (KJV) *If we confess our sins, he is faithful and just to forgive us our sins, and to cleanse us from all unrighteousness.*

However, receiving salvation equals freedom or right to eat of the children's bread of deliverance. Note that self-examination to deliverance is equivalent to freedom from bondage.

In an act of deliverance, the following must be acknowledged:

Salvation – deliverance of one's spirit

© Copyright All Rights Reserved. Joshua Ministries Int'l. Principles Of Deliverance

Liberation- freedom from being under control

Deliverance Vocabulary:

In the act of deliverance, there are certain words that are used such as:

- Freedom or set free from stronghold

- Loosed - Being released from holds of bondage

- Delivered – Jesus' blood produces remission of sins

- Rescue - Recovery from Satan's hold

- Save - Deliverance through the act of salvation

- Escape - deliver from curses (Galatians 3:13)

© Copyright All Rights Reserved. Joshua Ministries Int'l. Principles Of Deliverance

The Capabilities of Deliverance

Deliverance can be achieved through speaking. Deliverance is voice operated. Psalm 107:20 (KJV) *He sent his word, and healed them, and delivered them from their destructions.* It can also be achieved through seeking the Lord. Psalm 34:4 (KJV) *I sought the Lord, and he heard me, and delivered me from all my fears.*

Deliverance has the ability to take control over every satanic kingdom including the second heaven where principalities and satanic power reside. The act of deliverance can also free one's physical body from any form of sickness. There is no limit to what God can do through deliverance. Deliverance helps you regain complete control over your life. The absence of demonic control allows you to have liberty to make the right choices that you could not make freely. When delivered, you receive complete freedom to serve Jesus Christ, the only

23
© Copyright All Rights Reserved. Joshua Ministries Int'l. Principles Of Deliverance

true and living God, wholeheartedly and are no longer Satan's puppet.

Deliverance breaks the connection from the former life and leads you to the life made new in Christ Jesus. However, one can be delivered but still be walking in the influence of the former life. There are certain habits or character flaws that must be consciously dropped for the person to walk in the fullness of a new life in Christ Jesus.

Deliverance resets the clock of your life by freeing you from the bondage of sin and death. Romans 6:23 (KJV) *For the wages of sin is death; but the gift of God is eternal life through Christ Jesus our Lord. The* idea of sin is to shorten your life. John 10:10 (KJV) *The thief cometh not, but for to steal, and to kill, and to destroy: I am come that they might have life, and that they might have it more abundantly.* Here you can see what Satan's plan is. Through the act of deliverance though your clock is reset. You are now able to receive the life that God promises you in abundance

24

© Copyright All Rights Reserved. Joshua Ministries Int'l. Principles Of Deliverance

because you are no longer bound by the bondage of your former life.

Fear is a major weapon of the Kingdom of darkness and it is used to intimidate or prevent faith from operating or performing its duty.

The Acronym for FEAR is:

F - False

E - Evidence

A - Appearing

R – Real

© Copyright All Rights Reserved. Joshua Ministries Int'l. Principles Of Deliverance

All Believers Should Be Able to Perform Deliverance

Jesus clearly spoke about having the spirit of God upon Him to perform deliverance.

Luke 4:18 (KJV) *The Spirit of the Lord is upon me, because he hath anointed me to preach the gospel to the poor; he hath sent me to heal the brokenhearted, to preach deliverance to the captives, and recovering of sight to the blind, to set at liberty them that are bruised, To preach the acceptable year of the Lord.*

All believers must have the Holy Spirit operating on the inside of them before they engage in performing deliverance. It is the Holy Spirit which strengthens and empowers believers to carry out this spiritual duty.

Mark 16: 17 And these signs shall follow them that believe; In my name shall they cast out devils; they shall speak with new tongues;

First sign of believers is the ability to cast out devils (demons) in Jesus name. Declaration of Christ began by

26
© Copyright All Rights Reserved. Joshua Ministries Int'l. Principles Of Deliverance

bringing a clear understanding that we need the Holy Spirit

to perform deliverance.

© Copyright All Rights Reserved. Joshua Ministries Int'l. Principles Of
Deliverance

The Power of the Holy Spirit

We as believers must understand how and who gave us the power to cast out demons. The Holy Spirit uses us to transmit the power of God to establish God's Kingdom here on Earth. We can only wage a good war when we are empowered by the Holy Spirit. We must avail ourselves to be used by the Holy Spirit as believers. The Holy Spirit also acts as a GPS system to navigate us to the areas of a person's life where demons inhabit or are lodged to break the chains of bondage from the individual's life. The power of the Holy Spirit does far more than we could imagine; the Holy Spirit does a complete work.

Ephesians 3:20 (KJV) *Now unto him that is able to do exceeding abundantly above all that we ask or think, according to the power that worketh in us,*

Therefore, the Holy Spirit has a job or duty to perform which is to go beyond what we ask or think.

© Copyright All Rights Reserved. Joshua Ministries Int'l. Principles Of Deliverance

Acts 1:8 *But you will receive power when the Holy Spirit comes on you; and you will be my witnesses in Jerusalem, and in all Judea and Samaria, and to the ends of the earth.*

We need the fulfilment of the Holy Spirit to establish a good warfare. Acts 19:1-6 shows the importance of being filled with the Holy Spirit and what happens when the Holy Spirit comes. Acts 10:38 shows how God anointed Jesus of Nazareth with the Holy Spirit and power, and how he went around doing good and healing all who were under the power of the devil, because God was with him. God gave us power over satanic strongholds and Christ came to free those that were weighed down and whom Satan hath exercised dominion over.

Where there is deliverance, blessings will be released in fullness. Deliverance is also the operation of God's Kingdom towards mankind. It also brings the judgement of God upon Satan's kingdom.

© Copyright All Rights Reserved. Joshua Ministries Int'l. Principles Of Deliverance

Matthew 12:28 (KJV) *But if I cast out devils by the Spirit of God, then the kingdom of God is come unto you.*

If we understood this scripture then we would definitely move to receive freedom from any demonic stronghold! When the kingdom of God comes it means nothing else is able to remain unless it is in alignment with God's Kingdom!

© Copyright All Rights Reserved. Joshua Ministries Int'l. Principles Of Deliverance

Receiving Power

As believers we must understand that all authority was given to Jesus Christ which means that power was also given to us over every demonic arena.

Matthew 28:18 (KJV) *And Jesus came and spake unto them, saying, All power is given unto me in heaven and in earth.*

Every time deliverance comes through a man or woman of God, it is the operation of God releasing his Kingdom upon the individual with the evidence of deliverance. Deliverance is one of the acts of God with man.

Matthew 12:28 (KJV) *But if I cast out devils by the Spirit of God, then the kingdom of God is come unto you.*

Luke 10:9 (KJV) *And heal the sick that are therein, and say unto them, The kingdom of God is come nigh unto you.*

Luke 10:10-11 *But into whatsoever city ye enter, and they receive you not, go your ways out into the streets of the same, and say, Even the very dust of your city, which*

© Copyright All Rights Reserved. Joshua Ministries Int'l. Principles Of Deliverance

cleaveth on us, we do wipe off against you: notwithstanding

be ye sure of this, that the kingdom of God is come nigh

unto you.

The ministry of deliverance also works to provide or release divine healings. There are many people suffering from the spirit of infirmity. What they need is deliverance to break the stronghold of the infirmity. As people of God, whatever is affecting your body negatively and causing you to be ill, is a spirit. God did not create the human body to be sick. Deliverance brings freedom in those areas that need healing.

© Copyright All Rights Reserved. Joshua Ministries Int'l. Principles Of Deliverance

The Manifested Power

When you receive power the next thing you must do is demonstrate, manifest or execute that power. This manifested power is the expression of the Kingdom of God; it produces physical evidence of what the power of God is able to do.

Romans 8:19 (KJV) *For the earnest expectation of the creature waiteth for the manifestation of the sons of God.* This scripture tells us as believers that all creation waits for us to manifest in the power of God by the spirit that is at work in us. We must manifest as children of God bringing glory to God and awareness of his Kingdom. The more we manifest as children of God the more we empower other believers to activate their authority. We must constantly seek to reproduce disciples of God in order to affect the world and destroy Satan's Kingdom.

John 14:12-14 (KJV) *Verily, verily, I say unto you, He that believeth on me, the works that I do shall he do also; and*

33

© Copyright All Rights Reserved. Joshua Ministries Int'l. Principles Of Deliverance

greater works than these shall he do; because I go unto my

Father. And whatsoever ye shall ask in my name, that will I

do, that the Father may be glorified in the Son. If ye shall

ask any thing in my name, I will do it,

God's will is for us to manifest greater works to do a

complete work here on earth. We must be constantly

seeking to discover what God will have us to do to

demonstrate and glorify His Kingdom.

Deliverance can be achieved, executed or carried out in

many ways. Once you have received the power of the Holy

Spirit, your entire being becomes a weapon to destroy the

Kingdom of darkness.

1. Demons respond to the word of God as well as the voice

of God's divine servant.

Demons have to obey a higher authority which is Christ

Jesus operating through you. Psalms 107 vs. 20 (KJV) *He*

sent his word, and healed them, and delivered them from   ·

their destructions. Here deliverance came through the word

34

© Copyright All Rights Reserved. Joshua Ministries Int'l. Principles Of
Deliverance

of God being spoken. Power of the Spoken word causes deliverance Matthew 8:16 (AMP) *When evening came, many who were demon-possessed were brought to him, and he drove out the spirits with a word and healed all the sick.* Mark 1:25 (KJV) *And Jesus rebuked him, saying, Hold thy peace, and come out of him.* Mark 5:8 (KJV) *For he said unto him, Come out of the man, thou unclean spirit.*

Deliverance can be achieved through seeking the Lord. Psalms 34:4 (KJV) *I sought the Lord, and he heard me, and delivered me from all my fears.*It is the authority of the Holy Ghost which commands every demonic spirit to leave its presiding habitat.

- Deliverance is carried out through prayer and fasting

    Prayer and fasting is another weapon used in God's kingdom to bring power and cause deliverance. Matthew 17:14-21(KJV) *And when they were come to the multitude, there came to him a certain man,*

© Copyright All Rights Reserved. Joshua Ministries Int'l. Principles Of Deliverance

kneeling down to him, and saying, Lord, have mercy on my son: for he is lunatic, and sore vexed: for ofttimes he falleth into the fire, and oft into the water. And I brought him to thy disciples, and they could not cure him. Then Jesus answered and said, O faithless and perverse generation, how long shall I be with you? How long shall I suffer you? Bring him hither to me. And Jesus rebuked the devil; and he departed out of him: and the child was cured from that very hour Then came the disciples to Jesus apart, and said, Why could not we cast him out? And Jesus said unto them, Because of your unbelief: for verily I say unto you, If ye have faith as a grain of mustard seed, ye shall say unto this mountain, Remove hence to yonder place; and it shall remove; and nothing shall be impossible unto you. Howbeit this kind goeth not out but by prayer and fasting.

© Copyright All Rights Reserved. Joshua Ministries Int'l. Principles Of Deliverance

The ways Jesus administrated deliverance toward individuals are described in the scriptures.

- Mark 5:1-20

- Luke 8:26-39

- Matthew 8:28-34

Jesus used His authority to bring deliverance by directly speaking to the demonic spirit as he commands it to, "come out."

The first step to deliverance is to identify the demon or the strongman in control and render it powerless through the authority of the Holy Spirit. That same Holy Spirit that is operating on the inside of you gives you the authority to speak confidently and with faith in God through Jesus Christ our Lord.

© Copyright All Rights Reserved. Joshua Ministries Int'l. Principles Of Deliverance

Power through Deliverance

The ministry of deliverance is also the ministry of restoration or rehabilitation. Restoration or rehabilitation seeks to bring you back to a state of normalcy in the physical and spiritual. When a person receives deliverance he or she also receives the power of choice.

Mark 5:15 (KJV) *And they come to Jesus, and see him that was possessed with the devil, and had the legion, sitting, and clothed, and in his right mind: and they were afraid.*

Deliverance also brings awareness to society. This young man's deliverance brought a sense of recognition or witnessing of Jesus' Ministry.

Mark 5:19-20 (KJV) *Howbeit Jesus suffered him not, but saith unto him, Go home to thy friends, and tell them how great things the Lord hath done for thee, and hath had compassion on thee. And he departed, and began to publish in Decapolis how great things Jesus had done for him: and all men did marvel.*

© Copyright All Rights Reserved. Joshua Ministries Int'l. Principles Of Deliverance

We need more men and women of God to be raised up and to operate in the Ministry of Deliverance which is a gift to the church.

Deliverance causes freedom of one's spirit, for it is through our spirit God communicates. If the spirit is bound, communication between God and an individual cannot occur. Communication is power! Deliverance is God's great force against the Kingdom of darkness. This ministry of deliverance puts pressure on the devil's army.

© Copyright All Rights Reserved. Joshua Ministries Int'l. Principles Of Deliverance

Who Do We Wrestle Against?

2 Corinthians 10:3-4 (KJV):

> *For though we walk in the flesh, we do not war after*
>
> *the flesh: (For the weapons of our warfare are not*
>
> *carnal, but mighty through God to the pulling down*
>
> *of strong holds;)*

Deliverance is misunderstood greatly in this area. Our fight is not against or should not be against human beings (flesh) but after the spirit or spiritual beings. We must understand clearly that in order for demons to survive they need human bodies to work through. These human bodies gives Satan and his demons legal rights to have dominion.

These rights can be given through acts of:

- immoral living
- ancestral sins or iniquities that were done but never addressed through repentance and deliverance
- Witchcraft Practices

© Copyright All Rights Reserved. Joshua Ministries Int'l. Principles Of Deliverance

- Involvement in the occults

- False religious involvement

- Sacrifice or demonic worship

- hidden sins (murder, homosexuality, pornography viewing)

- Child sacrifices

- Offering up lands, house, monies as an evil offering

There are many more but anything that goes outside the law or right of God gives Satan access to inhabit individuals.

2 Corinthians 10:5 (KJV) *Casting down imaginations, and every high thing that exalteth itself against the knowledge of God, and bringing into captivity every thought to the obedience of Christ;*

Ephesians 6:12 (KJV) *For we wrestle not against flesh and blood, but against principalities, against powers, against the rulers of the darkness of this world, against spiritual wickedness in high places.*

© Copyright All Rights Reserved. Joshua Ministries Int'l. Principles Of Deliverance

The word 'wrestle', according to researched dictionaries means:

- To contend by grappling with and striving to trip or throw an opponent down or off balance

- To combat an opposing tendency or force (wrestling with conscience)

- To engage in deep thought, consideration, or debate

- To engage in or as if in a violent or determined struggle (wrestle with cumbersome luggage)

Every day we are faced with the various tactics used in the Kingdom of darkness. Satan's major plan is to steal, kill and destroy. This is his assignment toward God's children.

John 10:10 (KJV) *The thief cometh not, but for to steal, and to kill, and to destroy: I am come that they might have life, and that they might have it more abundantly.*

Many believers were taught they have no need to go through deliverance because they were set free through the act of salvation. This is true as salvation is the first act of

42

© Copyright All Rights Reserved. Joshua Ministries Int'l. Principles Of Deliverance

being set free from having Satan as the lord of your life. The actual act of deliverance sets you free from the sins of your past and their strongholds.

Galatians 3:13 (KJV) *Christ hath redeemed us from the curse of the law, being made a curse for us: for it is written, Cursed is every one that hangeth on a tree:*

Sometimes, we wrestle with the spirit of religion and that which we were accustomed to. During our wrestle we become blinded and unable to receive the ministry to operate in the gift of deliverance.

© Copyright All Rights Reserved. Joshua Ministries Int'l. Principles Of Deliverance

Signs of Curses and Symbols

Spirit of Asmodeus – This usually works with sickness and infirmity to affect the body. It is essential to cast this spirit out before healing can take place.

Sign of demonic curse and their functions and symbols.

There are six major problems which are curses and are evident in people's life.

1. Serious marital problems

2. Chronic sickness

3. Mental sickness

4. Serious financial problems

5. Repeated miscarriages

6. Being accident-prone

Many times we are experiencing some form of these activities which we may look at as a normal way of life; but, they are so dangerous to us and may even become generational curses.

© Copyright All Rights Reserved. Joshua Ministries Int'l. Principles Of Deliverance

In Nahum 3:4-19 Satan uses six different curses to cause confusion of the mind, demonic control and manipulation which causes failure of our faith.

© Copyright All Rights Reserved. Joshua Ministries Int'l. Principles Of Deliverance

Demonic Chains, Locations and Hiding Places

Webster Dictionary describes "chains" as "a series of things linked, connected, or associated together".

Commanding demons use this defense of protection to secure their legal rights by releasing a lower ranked demon to fool persons of deliverance to stop or prohibit real deliverance from being administered. This is how chains are protected from being destroyed. Demons often link together to form demonic chains. There can be more than one demonic chain operating in an individual's life. Each chain has a number of spirits with different ranks of authority. When administering deliverance, command the chains to be broken as well as the demonic networks. For example, you may have the spirit of fear working along with the spirit of lust, which is working with the spirit of condemnation, which is working with the spirit of depression, and the spirit of depression with the spirit of

© Copyright All Rights Reserved. Joshua Ministries Int'l. Principles Of Deliverance

gluttony, and the spirit of gluttony working with the spirit of shame.

Satan's mission and purpose is written in John 10:10. These chain demons work also like grouping spirits with each one corresponding with each other to formulate a chain of control.

© Copyright All Rights Reserved. Joshua Ministries Int'l. Principles Of Deliverance

Dealing With Sins to Break Chains

1. We must walk in submission: James 4:7 – There must be total submission to God and resisting the devil's temptation of corruption.

2. Confess sins and take responsibility for every act.

3. Ask God's forgiveness - repentance must be made. Psalms 51: 1-12 (iniquity, transgressions and sins) – King David counted himself responsible to break chains. We must be totally honest with God.

4. Seek help from Godly authority

5. Say a prayer of repentance and recommit your life to Christ after deliverance has been performed. Prayer and recommitting your life destroys Satan's legal right of having control in your life. Receiving the Holy Ghost and using the blood of Jesus also prevents you from being chained again by demons which were already cast out. An example from the Word of God is Matthew 12:43-45.

© Copyright All Rights Reserved. Joshua Ministries Int'l. Principles Of Deliverance

6. Declare and break every remaining links of chains of demonic interference

7. Use your authority binding and loosing spirits of the past

8. Cast out any residue in your soul

9. Ask the Holy Ghost to baptize and fill you with his power

10. Become accountable to leaders and eldership of a local church; do not forsake the assembly of God.

© Copyright All Rights Reserved. Joshua Ministries Int'l. Principles Of Deliverance

Demonic Locations

Demons will always attempt to hide in an individual. It is important not only to know the names of demons but also their locations. They can be located in the mind, the will, the emotions, the conscience or memory. These areas make up the soulish man. They can hide in the heart and different parts of the body, such as the blood, the bones, (particularly the back), muscles, eyes, ears, speech, tongue, sexual character, and appetite. They can hide in the systems of the body such as the nervous system, respiratory system, endocrine system, circulatory system, and digestive system. It is important to be led by the Holy Spirit to call out these evil spirits from a person's life. Demons will be in these areas of a person's body for years without being exposed until someone with an anointing can trouble their nest. They must be cast out. Some sicknesses cannot be healed without the demons being cast out or dismissed by God's chosen vessel.

© Copyright All Rights Reserved. Joshua Ministries Int'l. Principles Of Deliverance

The name of the spirit may also reflect or tell the location of the spirit. Call out the spirit with the authority of the Holy Ghost so that you can see the evidence of it being provoked out of its legal grounds. Whatever caused the demon to be there, gives it its legal rights or stronghold. Some demons are territorial. Their name gives them rank of position in the army of darkness.

© Copyright All Rights Reserved. Joshua Ministries Int'l. Principles Of Deliverance

How Demons Evacuate

Demons are manifested or evacuated through the avenue of coughing, drooling, vomiting, spitting, foaming, crying, screaming, sighing, roaring, belching, yawning, exhaling, etc. When demons are cast out normally they leave through the mouth or nose. Spirits are associated with breathing. Both the Hebrew and the Greek have two words for spirit and breath – Pneuma. Pneuma is an Ancient Greek word for breath, includes spirit, wind; related to blow, and breath. The other word for breath is Ruach - which means wind, breath, spirit. Evil spirits are exhaled sometimes during deliverance. An example is seen in John 20:22 (KJV) *And when he had said this, he breathed on them, and saith unto them, Receive ye the Holy Ghost:*

© Copyright All Rights Reserved. Joshua Ministries Int'l. Principles Of Deliverance

How to Identify Demons

Some of the manifestations of demons may be strange but it is through their manifestations that the root cause of how they entered is identified sometimes. For instance:

1. Demons of pornography may manifest by a person squinting his eyes – The person finds it hard to open his/her eyes but this also could indicate a spirit of lust of the eyes or of pornography.

2. Many times a person having a runny nose may indicate a spirit of lust.

3. When the eyes roll up in the person's eye sockets, it shows or indicates some form of involvement with occultism or witchcraft.

4. If there is gazing of the eyes, it may symbolise occultism or demon possession or ownership by demonic strongholds.

© Copyright All Rights Reserved. Joshua Ministries Int'l. Principles Of Deliverance

5. When a person's hands shape like animal claws it may symbolise witchcraft or murdering spirits in operation.

6. The spirit of masturbation manifests very strangely. Persons may have stiffness or rigidity in their hands, fingers or even their legs. These are signs and manifestation of masturbation.

7. Serpent spirits manifest by movements of a person's tongue. These can also be acts of the python spirit or a spirit of oral sex, homosexuality, lesbianism, depravity. This serpent spirit or python spirit works by controlling where it wraps itself around the individual making him/her become his prey or slave to his commands. It also works through leviathan.

The manifestation of a mocking spirit is with rude laughter, outburst or a smirking face. The spirit of shame may manifest by a person covering his/her face when being

© Copyright All Rights Reserved. Joshua Ministries Int'l. Principles Of Deliverance

delivered. Hiding or being unresponsive brings a spirit of

denial and self-rejection or even hatred and blame.

© Copyright All Rights Reserved. Joshua Ministries Int'l. Principles Of
Deliverance

How, When and Why Demons Enter

1. Before birth or in the mother's womb – Demons may enter an individual through rejection by parents or by them splitting up before the birth of the baby. Sometimes fathers may leave the mother after the birth of the child. Consequently, the child may feel fatherless giving grounds for the spirit of depression and rejection to inhabit that child.

2. A woman may hate her pregnancy –rejecting the child in her womb.

3. If a child is conceived through the act of fornication or wedlock this creates an open door for demons to enter. This opens the child up to the spirit of the bastard.

4. If a child is conceived through an adulterous affair, the child is therefore born under a curse through the avenue of immoral living of the parents, which may be passed on from generation to generation.

© Copyright All Rights Reserved. Joshua Ministries Int'l. Principles Of Deliverance

5. Sins committed without any form of repentance or ancestral sins such as through witchcraft involvement gives access for demons to enter.

6. Human sacrifice of children or blood given to witches and/or warlocks to perform rituals of devil worship creates access.

7. Plans of abortion can open the door for the spirit of murder to enter the mother as well as the child.

8. Involvement in another man's sin can open a door way for demon possession.

9. Unfaithful confessions; Proverbs 18:21 (KJV) *Death and life are in the power of the tongue: and they that love it shall eat the fruit thereof.*

10. Willful sinning or defiling God's temple which is your body by joining in or entangling yourself with sexual sin also creates an open door. This is shown below in:

© Copyright All Rights Reserved. Joshua Ministries Int'l. Principles Of Deliverance

2 Corinthians 6:14-18 (KJV) *Be ye not unequally yoked together with unbelievers: for what fellowship hath righteousness with unrighteousness? and what communion hath light with darkness?And what concord hath Christ with Belial? or what part hath he that believeth with an infidel? And what agreement hath the temple of God with idols? for ye are the temple of the living God; as God hath said, I will dwell in them, and walk in them; and I will be their God, and they shall be my people. Wherefore come out from among them, and be ye separate, saith the Lord, and touch not the unclean thing; and I will receive you. And will be a Father unto you, and ye shall be my sons and daughters, saith the Lord Almighty.*

Remember to be very careful of who and what you are connected to as children of God. As believers we carry the atmosphere of the Kingdom of God, just as those without God carry the atmosphere of Satan, which is darkness.

© Copyright All Rights Reserved. Joshua Ministries Int'l. Principles Of Deliverance

How to Deal with Demons: Spiritual warfare and weapons of actions against demons.

Tools of Deliverance

1. Self examination by the Word of God.

2. Prayerful lifestyle –as believers we must always be in constant communication with God.

3. Having a fast lifestyle – emptiness before God brings fullness of the Holy Spirit.

4. Possess a submissive spirit to leaders in authority.

5. Possess a teachable spirit – this causes humility. It is a plus or bonus in warfare because it allows the Holy Spirit to equip you and teach you new weapons of warfare.

6. Sober mind – God cannot work with an unstable mind. A sober mind brings balance to every area of one's life.

7. Servant's heart – this is the beginning of greatness.

© Copyright All Rights Reserved. Joshua Ministries Int'l. Principles Of Deliverance

8. Humble spirit – this is the seed for meekness.

9. Heart of Love –this demonstrates the power of God.

10. Caring for others is a great tool of success.

These tools when used properly will conquer and render Satan's kingdom powerless. They will also help you to wage a good warfare against the Kingdom of darkness. Deliverance should not be based upon your strength but the strength of the Holy Spirit of God while you remain submissive to his leadership and his weapon of choice.

Tools of Warfare

The greatest weapon is love. When we as believers can demonstrate love to someone who is demonically depressed or possessed, this shows the love and mercy of God and His Kingdom.

Matthew 12:25 – 29 (KJV):

> *And Jesus knew their thoughts, and said unto them,*
> *Every kingdom divided against itself is brought to*
> *desolation; and every city or house divided against*

© Copyright All Rights Reserved. Joshua Ministries Int'l. Principles Of Deliverance

itself shall not stand: And if Satan cast out Satan, he is divided against himself; how shall then his kingdom stand? And if I by Beelzebub cast out devils, by whom do your children cast them out? therefore they shall be your judges. But if I cast out devils by the Spirit of God, then the kingdom of God is come unto you. Or else how can one enter into a strong man's house, and spoil his goods, except he first bind the strong man? and then he will spoil his house.

When dealing with demon possessed people, one must take control over the strongman or the ruling spirit which is giving commands. The strongman also makes groups or chains that make links in an individual's life.

© Copyright All Rights Reserved. Joshua Ministries Int'l. Principles Of Deliverance

Keys for Rendering the Strongman Powerless

- Identify the demon by name.

- Determine the type of demon that is involved

- Locate the strongman through the blood, whether the strongman is in the mind, body or soul.

- Find out how the demon gained legal rights to enter and possess or oppress.

- Discover what the operation of the demon is.

- Inquire if the person afflicted himself/herself causing the demon to enter.

- Determine whether the strongman came through ancestral sins like acts of witchcraft, demonic pledges and human sacrifices.

- Uncover unforgiveness which gives access to tormenting spirits.

- Ascertain the source of possession for instance through acts of rape, incest, sodomy, homosexual relationships, lesbianism, visiting a witchcraft or

© Copyright All Rights Reserved. Joshua Ministries Int'l. Principles Of Deliverance

bush doctor, involvement in occult practices, palm readings, nature worship and psychic hotline.

One must repent from the involvement or confess the iniquities of one's sinful acts and take responsibility for the decision made in life. It is necessary to repent on behalf of deceased family members for their involvement in witchcraft and sorcery before you were even conceived, so that you can receive the benefits of deliverance through the blood of Jesus Christ.

John 21:25 (KJV) *And there are also many other things which Jesus did, the which, if they should be written every one, I suppose that even the world itself could not contain the books that should be written. Amen.*

The Bible highlights that there were many things that Jesus performed that were not recorded because there are not enough books.

© Copyright All Rights Reserved. Joshua Ministries Int'l. Principles Of Deliverance

Demons Attack the Mind

2 Corinthians 10 vs. 4-5 (KJV) *(For the weapons of our warfare are not carnal, but mighty through God to the pulling down of strong holds;) Casting down imaginations, and every high thing that exalteth itself against the knowledge of God, and bringing into captivity every thought to the obedience of Christ;*

Most demons gain their stronghold by attacking the mind by releasing lustful thoughts. The mind will be pressured which will cause lust to control a person's will. In doing so, it causes the person to give in to the feelings he or she may have at that moment and commit sexually immoral sins with his or her body. It also uses thoughts of murder, especially when a person experiences rejection, lust, abandonment from someone he/she loves or even trusts with his/her feelings. The mind is a battlefield where all kinds of thoughts will come your way. Apostle Paul warns believers in Romans 12: 1-2 not to allow the ways of this

64

© Copyright All Rights Reserved. Joshua Ministries Int'l. Principles Of Deliverance

world to shape our lifestyles by renewing our minds which is key to living and maintaining a victorious life.

Romans 12 vs. 1-2 (KJV): *I beseech you therefore, brethren, by the mercies of God, that ye present your bodies a living sacrifice, holy, acceptable unto God, which is your reasonable service. And be not conformed to this world: but be ye transformed by the renewing of your mind, that ye may prove what is that good, and acceptable, and perfect, will of God.* Satan will also attack your mind causing you to think highly of yourself. Apostle Paul even warns us about that, stating that it is a weapon of darkness that can cultivate pridefulness.

Romans 12:3 (KJV) *For I say, through the grace given unto me, to every man that is among you, not to think of himself more highly than he ought to think; but to think soberly,*

© Copyright All Rights Reserved. Joshua Ministries Int'l. Principles Of Deliverance

according as God hath dealt to every man the measure of faith.

Be conscious and alert of what you allow in your thoughts; you must keep your mind on good Godly thoughts. When you allow Satan to attack your mind, your focus is on things which do not help your soulish man to prosper. This can also cause harm to your abilities to make proper judgement for your life. This is why Apostle Paul made these statements in Philippians 4 vs. 8-9.

Philippians 4: 8-9 (KJV) *Finally, brethren, whatsoever things are true, whatsoever things are honest, whatsoever things are just, whatsoever things are pure, whatsoever things are lovely, whatsoever things are of good report; if there be any virtue, and if there be any praise, think on these things. Those things, which ye have both learned, and received, and heard, and seen in me, do: and the God of peace shall be with you.*

© Copyright All Rights Reserved. Joshua Ministries Int'l. Principles Of Deliverance

We must truly learn to guard our minds from what comes in the gates of our souls. Satan will attack those areas of gates to our soul.

- The gate to your eye – what you see.

- The gate to your ear – what you listen to.

- The gate to your mouth – what you say.

All these openings are connected to one's soul.

Condemnation

The enemy uses your past to attack your mind. According to Romans 8:1(KJV) *There is therefore now no condemnation to them which are in Christ Jesus, who walk not after the flesh, but after the Spirit.*

We must not allow the enemy to bring back our past mistakes to us. The blood of Jesus should be used against him to resist him and he will flee from us. Use the Word, the Blood and the Cross against the devil. Mind attacks stop by using these weapons of the Kingdom of God.

© Copyright All Rights Reserved. Joshua Ministries Int'l. Principles Of Deliverance

James 4:7-8 (KJV) *Submit yourselves therefore to God. Resist the devil, and he will flee from you. Draw nigh to God, and he will draw nigh to you. Cleanse your hands, ye sinners; and purify your hearts, ye double minded.*

Luke 4: 1-14 (KJV)

[1]And Jesus being full of the Holy Ghost returned from Jordan, and was led by the Spirit into the wilderness, Being forty days tempted of the devil. And in those days he did eat nothing: and when they were ended, he afterward hungered. And the devil said unto him, If thou be the Son of God, command this stone that it be made bread. And Jesus answered him, saying, It is written, That man shall not live by bread alone, but by every word of God. And the devil, taking him up into a high mountain, shewed unto him all the kingdoms of the world in a moment of time. And the devil said unto him, All this

© Copyright All Rights Reserved. Joshua Ministries Int'l. Principles Of Deliverance

power will I give thee, and the glory of them: for that is delivered unto me; and to whomsoever I will I give it. If thou therefore wilt worship me, all shall be thine. And Jesus answered and said unto him, Get thee behind me, Satan: for it is written, Thou shalt worship the Lord thy God, and him only shalt thou serve. And he brought him to Jerusalem, and set him on a pinnacle of the temple, and said unto him, If thou be the Son of God, cast thyself down from hence: For it is written, He shall give his angels charge over thee, to keep thee: And in their hands they shall bear thee up, lest at any time thou dash thy foot against a stone. And Jesus answering said unto him, It is said, Thou shalt not tempt the Lord thy God. And when the devil had ended all the temptation, he departed from him for a season. And Jesus returned in the power of the Spirit into

© Copyright All Rights Reserved. Joshua Ministries Int'l. Principles Of Deliverance

Galilee: and there went out a fame of him through

all the region round about.

© Copyright All Rights Reserved. Joshua Ministries Int'l. Principles Of
Deliverance

Prayer For the Mind

How to use this Prayer as guidance

Start by praising God and giving thanks to Him. Confess any sin you may remember by asking the Holy Spirit to examine your heart. Use the blood of Jesus to cleanse your body, soul, mind and spirit and focus on accepting your forgiveness according to 1 John 1: 9-10 by receiving by faith.

The Prayer

"Father, I approach your throne through the blood of Jesus Christ. I receive now, all the good benefits that came through the shedding of your blood in Jesus' name. I take authority over all attacks of my mind in Jesus' name. I cancel Satan's attack on my mind. Lord, I receive the same mind of Jesus Christ. Everything that exalted itself in my mind. I now plead the blood of Jesus in my mind and soul and I receive purification in my mind. Every imagination

© Copyright All Rights Reserved. Joshua Ministries Int'l. Principles Of Deliverance

that comes in my mind, I cast it down and I stand on the Word of God. I refuse to receive anything from the Kingdom of darkness in Jesus' name. I declare my mind is free in Jesus' name, Amen!"

Start thanking God for your freedom. Continue to praise and worship until you feel release in your body.

The mind is where the war is. Your thoughts govern your actions. You can be brain dead physically and still be alive and breathing, same way spiritually. Once your mind is bound it is as if you are dead but alive because you are being controlled by Satan. Society has slapped a name on people who are negatively affected in their minds to cushion the truth. The truth is demons or spirits sit upon the head like the squid and the octopus to lead a person into complete demise. However, through the power of deliverance God is able to set the mind free and give a person total control again!

© Copyright All Rights Reserved. Joshua Ministries Int'l. Principles Of Deliverance

The Human Spirit

The human spirit of the will is a spirit of pride and rebellion. Many times when a person cannot be delivered, it is because a strong will is refusing to submit to the leading of the Holy Ghost and he/she does not know how to let go of self. We can know how this spirit operates by reading Isaiah 14:12-14.

How art thou fallen from heaven, O Lucifer, son of the morning! how art thou cut down to the ground, which didst weaken the nations! For thou hast said in thine heart, I will ascend into heaven, I will exalt my throne above the stars of God: I will sit also upon the mount of the congregation, in the sides of the north: I will ascend above the heights of the clouds; I will be like the most High.

These scriptures show how lucifer was operating on himself. Look carefully at how many times he used "I" which symbolizes a prideful, rebellious nature.

© Copyright All Rights Reserved. Joshua Ministries Int'l. Principles Of Deliverance

This spirit is one spirit that can truly hinder or prevent deliverance. This spirit can also keep you outside of the will of God like lucifer. He had to be kicked out of heaven which made him lose his position in heaven.

This spirit may cause a person to become self-existent, requiring no one's help in life. It may even cause a person to exalt himself/herself during deliverance. When this human spirit is in operation, it seeks to draw attention to itself. This may be done through expressing how great he/she is, giving the impression that it is a demonic spirit speaking. This human spirit will even go as far as to call itself a prophet. Another example is the person voicing some hurt inflicted upon him/her from a particular church or church leader. For example, the deliverance minister might hear the person say " I was hurt by the church." The person performing this deliverance must quickly bring this person to an awareness that he/she is operating in this spirit

© Copyright All Rights Reserved. Joshua Ministries Int'l. Principles Of Deliverance

and that it can affect his/her deliverance. The deliverance

coordinator must not be afraid to firmly stop this act of self.

© Copyright All Rights Reserved. Joshua Ministries Int'l. Principles Of Deliverance

Myths of Deliverance

The lack of knowledge in relation to deliverance has lent itself to the creation and cultivation of the myths and fictional teaching in deliverance ministries. Therefore, light must be shed on the true elements surrounding deliverance. These myths include:

- Only a special minister (priest, pastor) can perform deliverance - This statement is far from the truth, remember Mark 16:17 (KJV) *And these signs shall follow them that believe; In my name shall they cast out devils; they shall speak with new tongues;* for everyone that believes. Every single person regardless of their age or race can perform deliverance simply by their belief in God! However, what you must have is the baptism of the Holy Ghost!

- Demons leave only by manifesting- A person is set free in many ways. There is no one special way that

© Copyright All Rights Reserved. Joshua Ministries Int'l. Principles Of Deliverance

demons must leave. The woman with the issue of blood having a spirit of infirmity experienced deliverance by just touching the helm of God's garment. Did she manifest? Did she vomit or fall out? No, but she was healed! This clearly showed that she was free from demonic stronghold. Manifestation does not mean a person is delivered!

- You go to hell if you do not go through deliverance/ have demons cast out – This needs to be properly explained but it's simple. The first act of deliverance is really accepting Jesus Christ as Lord and Savior, renouncing Satan as lord over your life. Remember also sin does not send you to hell but not accepting Christ does. However, if a person has accepted Christ but did not receive an opportunity to experience deliverance he or she will still be candidates for heaven. He or she has completed the first act of having deliverance of one's soul through

© Copyright All Rights Reserved. Joshua Ministries Int'l. Principles Of Deliverance

salvation. God wants us to receive the total benefits of His grace which includes deliverance from any demonic activity which may function in a believer who doesn't know his or her heavenly rights as sons of God. The gift of deliverance is given to the church body.

© Copyright All Rights Reserved. Joshua Ministries Int'l. Principles Of Deliverance

What Happens After Deliverance

Maintaining Deliverance

Maintaining (preserving, protecting, keeping or upholding) your deliverance is just as important as partaking in the bread of deliverance. We must guard our deliverance with all our heart to continually reap the benefits of freedom. Maintaining our deliverance is no different from when we fix something that was broken. We then put measures in place to prevent it from being broken again. We must put measures in place to remain free from bondage.

Galatians 5:1 (KJV) *Stand fast therefore in the liberty wherewith Christ hath made us free, and be not entangled again with the yoke of bondage.*

This scripture bids us not to return to bondage that came through sin after we have been set free. One definite method of maintaining deliverance is becoming completely knowledgeable of the schemes and tactics that Satan uses to re-entangle us.

© Copyright All Rights Reserved. Joshua Ministries Int'l. Principles Of Deliverance

Hosea 4:6 (KJV) *My people are destroyed for lack of knowledge…*

The Bible educates us on what happens after a demon is cast out.

Matthew 12:43-45

When the unclean spirit is gone out of a man, he walketh through dry places, seeking rest, and findeth none. Then he saith, I will return into my house from whence I came out; and when he is come, he findeth it empty, swept, and garnished.

The spirit that walks through dry places is called the strongman. This is the demon that has a very tight grip in a person's life. After it has been cast out it seeks a place of rest and if it finds none. It returns to the person from which it came from. If that person has not filled the empty space which the spirit left that strongman returns to live again and entangle that life again.

© Copyright All Rights Reserved. Joshua Ministries Int'l. Principles Of Deliverance

Then goeth he, and taketh with himself seven other spirits more wicked than himself, and they enter in and dwell there: and the last state of the man is worse than the first. Even so shall it be also unto this wicked generation.

However, that strong man does not just live there alone. He brings others that are stronger than himself in order to rule your life and keep the help of God's Holy Spirit out. The spirit becomes a strong man when we open ourselves again to unclean works.

Galatians 5:16-17 (KJV)

This I say then, Walk in the Spirit, and ye shall not fulfil the lust of the flesh. For the flesh lusteth against the Spirit, and the Spirit against the flesh: and these are contrary the one to the other: so that ye cannot do the things that ye would.

You cannot protect your freedom if you continually walk in the fruits of the flesh according to Galatians 5:19-21 (KJV)

© Copyright All Rights Reserved. Joshua Ministries Int'l. Principles Of Deliverance

Now the works of the flesh are manifest, which are these;

Adultery, fornication, uncleanness, lasciviousness, Idolatry,

witchcraft, hatred, variance, emulations, wrath, strife,

seditions, heresies, Envyings, murders, drunkenness,

revellings, and such like: of the which I tell you before, as I

have also told you in time past, that they which do such

things shall not inherit the kingdom of God.

Instead, we must bear the fruits that are of God. That way

one's deliverance can be maintained as the scripture states

if we walk after the spirit of God, we will not fulfill the lust

or the desires of the flesh and the strong man cannot find

legal grounds to re-enter and take root again. The fruits of

the Spirit, according to Galatians 5:22-23 (KJV):

But the fruit of the Spirit is love, joy, peace, longsuffering,

gentleness, goodness, faith, Meekness, temperance: against

such there is no law.

© Copyright All Rights Reserved. Joshua Ministries Int'l. Principles Of
Deliverance

Satan also uses the spirit of religion to bring people into the entanglement of their soul. The religious spirit causes the brethren to hold new wine in old wine skin and not live a victorious life in Christ.

Galatians 5:2-4 (KJV) *Behold, I Paul say unto you, that if ye be circumcised, Christ shall profit you nothing.* (This refers to the spirit of religion or religious spirits)

For I testify again to every man that is circumcised, that he is a debtor to do the whole law. Christ is become of no effect unto you, whosoever of you are justified by the law; ye are fallen from grace.

Religion does not remember grace; it also keeps you from a relationship with God. In order to maintain your deliverance you must establish a true connection with God. You must learn and live in his ways and seek after his direction. Following after tradition and religion can create demonic restriction and barriers in your life.

© Copyright All Rights Reserved. Joshua Ministries Int'l. Principles Of Deliverance

James 4:7-8 (KJV) *Submit yourselves therefore to God.*

Resist the devil, and he will flee from you. Draw nigh to

God, and he will draw nigh to you. Cleanse your hands, ye

sinners; and purify your hearts, ye double minded.

Foster a relationship with God in order to resist or fight

against the devil and keep your mind free.

James 1:8 (KJV) *A double minded man is unstable in all*

his ways.

© Copyright All Rights Reserved. Joshua Ministries Int'l. Principles Of
Deliverance

Preparation for Self Deliverance

Deliverance of oneself is one of the secret weapons of the Kingdom of God. You as a believer have the right over your body, soul, and spirit. This portion of the book is so that all believers in Christ who wish to partake of the bread of self deliverance are successful in doing so. Self deliverance, however, is not fully recognized as a necessity within the body of Christ.

Find a quiet place or somewhere that you will not be disturbed or distracted from the process of self deliverance so that God can do a complete work in you.

The first step to receiving deliverance is acknowledging your sins before God; only an honest and sorrowful or repentant heart can receive full and true deliverance.

1 John- 1: 9-10 (KJV) *If we confess our sins, he is faithful and just to forgive us our sins, and to cleanse us from all unrighteousness. If we say that we have not sinned, we*

85

© Copyright All Rights Reserved. Joshua Ministries Int'l. Principles Of Deliverance

make him a liar, and his word is not in us.

We cannot fool God, He is the one that searches the heart.

All of us have sinned so be truthful and confess your sins

so you can be made whole.

Now that you understand what needs to be done before

deliverance just open you your heart and your spirit to be

set free from Satan's bondage. God promises He will not

reject a broken and contrite heart. He sees your heart needs

forgiveness so now simply ask him for forgiveness of your

sins.

Remember, deliverance is the children of God's bread so if

you do not know Jesus as your Lord and Savior, say this

simple prayer:

Lord, please forgive me of all my sins, come into my heart

and save me, I renounce Satan as lord over my life, Jesus is

my Lord and Savior now. I am born again now in Jesus

name amen.

© Copyright All Rights Reserved. Joshua Ministries Int'l. Principles Of Deliverance

I am so happy for you for what you have done; now you are

empowered by the life of Christ and the anointing from the

anointed one - Jesus is His name.

There are blockages toward self deliverance, where things

that we have done make the devil thinks he has legal rights

in our lives still. There are a number of things that need to

be addressed so that Satan cannot use them against you to

stop you from becoming totally delivered. These things

must be confessed, and denounced openly. Let the devil

hear you breaking the chains to your life by asking

forgiveness for each one of them, in Jesus name. These

things include repenting of

(1)Abortion

(2) Visiting witch doctor or any cultic activity any time in

your life

(3) Adultery or an adulterous affair.

© Copyright All Rights Reserved. Joshua Ministries Int'l. Principles Of
Deliverance

(4) Practicing any form of incest

(5) Holding any form of unforgiveness

Now forgive anyone who has hurt you and open your spirit for God's Kingdom to come upon you. You may need napkins or a bowl in preparation for when these demonic spirits are leaving your life. Remember to revert to the chapter that teaches about what is expected to happen in deliverance such as sneezing, coughing, burping, crying, screaming, etc. You can make a list of the spirits that may be disrupting your life such as

- Sickness of any kind

- Insomnia

- Mind control

- Barrenness

© Copyright All Rights Reserved. Joshua Ministries Int'l. Principles Of Deliverance

- Failure

- Joylessness

- Prayerlessness

- Financial struggles

Prayer of Self Deliverance

Now that you have repented of your sins and have told God you have come to be delivered you can say this prayer and carefully follow these instructions.

I declare every yoke of bondage which was placed on me from sins of my past, ancestral sins, generational curses be broken now in Jesus name. Every attack which came about from witchcraft receive fire from the third heaven in Jesus name. Every legal chains melt from heavenly fire in Jesus name. Anything and everything in my body I command you

89

© Copyright All Rights Reserved. Joshua Ministries Int'l. Principles Of Deliverance

to come out of me from wherever you entered me - through

my mouth, nose, eyes, ears or my sexual organ in Jesus

name. You spirit that came to me in my sleep be gone in

Jesus name.

The way God has anointed me to do deliverance may seem

different and strange but just follow these instructions step

by step. Five is the number of grace.

Inhale from your mouth and exhale five times. While doing

this, declare the Kingdom of God has come upon me to

deliver me.

On the fifth inhale, cough and keep coughing. Ensure that

you have a basin to receive whatever comes out of you. As

you cough command every spirit operating in you that you

know of - pain, illness, fatigue; everything bothering you

call it out and cough. Do not swallow! Allow yourself to be

purged completely.

© Copyright All Rights Reserved. Joshua Ministries Int'l. Principles Of
Deliverance

You can repeat the process until satisfied completely.

Yawning or crying are also apart of deliverance. However, these manifestations do not prove a person has received complete deliverance. The evidence of true deliverance is seen after. It is seen in your everyday life. It is seen through positive changes, signs of healing from an illness, or no longer engaging in any ungodly acts. Please note: temptation does not mean you are not delivered. Persistently resisting these temptations show that you are no longer bound by Satan's hold. Remember to cast out any demonic residue, mucus and let the Lord scrape you from inside.

At the end of your deliverance thank God for His power and healing and acknowledge that you have been set free. Cover your family, finances and your possessions under the blood of Jesus. When a person is being set free the enemy

© Copyright All Rights Reserved. Joshua Ministries Int'l. Principles Of Deliverance

will attempt to bring even more destruction because he

does not want your freedom to occur.

© Copyright All Rights Reserved. Joshua Ministries Int'l. Principles Of Deliverance

Identification of Demonic Vomits

This part of the book might be the most indifferent portion you will read. However, this is why this book was written to bring awareness to the body of Christ. You may ask, does vomit have meaning? The answer is yes. Vomit has different identities because of its colors and scents. However, over the years of doing deliverance and most of all by the leading of the Holy Spirit one is taught on the different manifestations and bahaviours of demons. Therefore, even vomit has a significant meaning in deliverance because it is a demonic manifestation.

The color of vomit as a result of deliverance has different colours.

When deliverance is taking place, you may observe vomit coming from a person's mouth and/or nose or that of yours if you are engaging in self deliverance. The vomit may be a bright red fluid giving the appearance of blood or sputum. The fluid may also be of a darker color red. This fluid or

© Copyright All Rights Reserved. Joshua Ministries Int'l. Principles Of Deliverance

liquid is in fact blood. However, do not be alarmed or fearful which may cause the act of deliverance to end prematurely although complete deliverance is necessary. One of the spirits behind blood-filled vomit is a murdering spirit. These manifestions of blood known as ancestral murder crimes came through primarily because of the following: If you did the act or had the intention to commit murder or have family members who have committed murder plus have experienced rejection. Deliverance is most definitely needed. Furthermore, this act causes a generational curse of murder to follow the family.It's possibly that family members may experience death through the avenue of murders in their lineage. This murdering, rejection spirits must be cast out from the family lineage through the power of God in Jesus name. The weapons for this warfare is without a doubt the bruised blood of Jesus Christ that was shed. To have complete deliverance you should say, "I release the bruised blood of

94
© Copyright All Rights Reserved. Joshua Ministries Int'l. Principles Of Deliverance

Jesus in the deep inner parts of (insert the individual's name) body, soul and spirit" or in your own parts and command the spirit of murder and rejection plus death to leave in Jesus name. This must be articulated forcefully to assert your authority. You may have to be loud. Say it like you are destroying something in front of you.

Another type of demonic vomit may appear black in color and carry a foul odour. The color black represents demonic poison in operation and or the spirit of witchcraft. This may seem strange and even difficult to understand but demons do release poison. One particular way is in dreams. If you find yourself eating food in a dream this may be a release of demonic poison. Identifying this spirit is very important particularly to avoid this person from being harmed or even experiencing death., A good indicator that demonic poison is in operation is when praying and commanding the spirit to come out of a person or yourself it seems as if the spirit is not moving and the person looks

95

© Copyright All Rights Reserved. Joshua Ministries Int'l. Principles Of Deliverance

like he or she is dying. This may also mean that

the person's soul has been damaged to an extent that he or

she cannot or may not be able to relate to you. This may

pose a challenge to cast out, but remember nothing is

impossible with God. Satan has already been put to an open

shame. Therefore, to deal with this spirit you must be

consistent in prayer and intercession. One may need to call

the prayer warriors of the church to assist in this type of

deliverance. If an individual is aware or even suspect that

he or she may have been demonically poisoned I suggest

deliverance be administered by someone filled with the

Holy Spirit. The individual seeking deliverance should not

attempt self deliverance in order to avoid unnecessary

harm. Another weapon of warfare in this type of

deliverance is the use of the blood of Jesus. Command the

spirit of demonic poison to vomit up in Jesus name. Also,

ensure you command demonic residue to come out in Jesus

name. Remember, it is pertinent that nothing remains.

96
© Copyright All Rights Reserved. Joshua Ministries Int'l. Principles Of
Deliverance

Demonic mucus, which may dwell in the walls of a person's stomach, must be called out of the person being delivered. Command this spirit to leave until you observe a change is occurring in this person; particularly full consciousness should be regained and this person should be able to relate to you.

Now, a mixture of colors of vomit can be the spirit of positions, meaning this person is being possessed by demons. This speaks of ownership of their soul. When more than one demon is in operation you must find the strongest one in operation. This is received only through the release of the Holy Spirit. Once the ruling demon or strong man is identified then the person doing the deliverance definitely has the upper hand and must cast this demon out along with its smaller demons.

Word of Knowledge is a great weapon to utilize to cast out these demons. The word of God declares ask and you shall receive. Do not neglect to listen to the voice of

© Copyright All Rights Reserved. Joshua Ministries Int'l. Principles Of Deliverance

God in deliverance or you can miss and make the process longer than it really needs to be. Therefore, patience is a very important part in this process.

James 4:2-3 (KJV) *Ye lust, and have not: ye kill, and desire to have, and cannot obtain: ye fight and war, yet ye have not, because ye ask not. Ye ask, and receive not, because ye ask amiss, that ye may consume it upon your lusts.*

All of your motives for asking of God must be clean and clear to God. He already knows the agenda of our hearts. Asking because you care for the life of an individual is very important and you who are performing deliverance must desire to see that person set free. All perfect gifts come from above, and God knows what we need before we ever ask. *Ask because of love and receive the power to cast out any demon.

James 1:17 (KJV) *Every good gift and every perfect gift is from above, and cometh down from the Father of lights, with whom is no variableness, neither shadow of turning.*

98

© Copyright All Rights Reserved. Joshua Ministries Int'l. Principles Of Deliverance

Another type of vomit you may experience through deliverance is one that is transparent or clear as water. Please, do not be fooled by this because you have not seen any dark color. This can be water spirits in action. This is where the big boys may be playing in that person's soul. In other words this may be marine spirits. Let me explain a little bit. The earth is surrounded by 70% water. Guess what this means? It means more territories for demons to rule and reign upon the Earth. The strongest part of the dark kingdom of Satan is the marine world. Here is where the devil and his strong forces love to operate. In the marine kingdom demons, like the queen of the second heaven, the queen of the coast lines, and leviathan the sea monster rule. These type of demons rule all the waters of the earth and their greatest attack comes through sexual perversion. About 80% of marital problems which may lead to divorce, comes through these types of spirit including incest, rape,

© Copyright All Rights Reserved. Joshua Ministries Int'l. Principles Of Deliverance

homosexuality, and lesbianism. These are all governed by the marine kingdom.

One of the weapons God taught me in this type of warfare is to suffocate these spirits by commanding all the oxygen to dry up in Jesus name. When a person appears to be choking, you must command the spirit to leave. As a deliverance minister you must be watching and listening because the physical is just as involved as the spiritual. When using this type of weapon of warfare that is drying up oxygen, a person will literally appear to be gasping for air even holding his or her throat. Once this observation is made, you must command the demon to not injure the person and command the person to come forward. Remember the word of God declares in John 10:10 *the devil comes to steal, kill and destroy.* Therefore, the enemy is not leaving without a fight.

Take full authority and command total dismissal to all the

© Copyright All Rights Reserved. Joshua Ministries Int'l. Principles Of Deliverance

marine spirits in Jesus name. If the demons refuse to leave, command the waters to dry up in Jesus name. This is another weapon of warfare I learnt through deliverance from the guidance of the Holy Spirit. When their waters are dried up, their legal grounds have been taken away. Call on the fire of the Holy Spirit to burn up everything in the water including the place where their headquarters is in Jesus name.

Now you know and understand, how and what different vomits mean, I hope you will be more effective in your deliverance journey in the Lord. God has taught me how to understand things we may have taken for granted and with this new awareness I can fight a better warfare and so can you. The Apostle Paul said, don't be ignorant of the devils devices, that is why as children of God we need to be educated about spiritual warfare against the kingdom of darkness.

© Copyright All Rights Reserved. Joshua Ministries Int'l. Principles Of Deliverance

2 Corinthians 2:11 (KJV) *Lest Satan should get an advantage of us: for we are not ignorant of his devices.*

You are now armed and dangerous to destroy the kingdom of darkness; you are more than a conqueror in Jesus name. God bless you!

© Copyright All Rights Reserved. Joshua Ministries Int'l. Principles Of Deliverance

About the Author

Apostle Dr. Glen England is the founder of Joshua Ministries International, a ministry that has birth many youth that are after the heart of God. Apostle Dr. Glen England is an international Apostle and Prophet that has a heart for bringing deliverance to all. Apostle England is called to speak to many nations around the world and bring divine healing and deliverance to the sick and the broken hearted.

Apostle England resides in the Caribbean island of Saint Kitts with his lovely wife and children.

© Copyright All Rights Reserved. Joshua Ministries Int'l. Principles Of Deliverance

Bibliography

- Hammond, Frank, and Ida Mae. Hammond. Pigs in the Parlour: A Practical Guide to Deliverance. Chichester: New Wine, 1992.

- Eckhardt, John, Apostle. Prayers That Rout Demons. Florida: Charisma House, 2007.

- Heward-Mills, D. (2006). Demons and how to deal with them. S.l.: Parchment House.

- Ramirez, J. (2011). Out Of the Devil's Cauldron. Alachua, Florida: Bridge Logos Foundation.

- Eckhardt, John. Deliverance Thesaurus: Demon Hit List. New Kensington, PA: Whitaker House, 2000.

© Copyright All Rights Reserved. Joshua Ministries Int'l. Principles Of Deliverance

© Copyright All Rights Reserved. Joshua Ministries Int'l. Principles Of
Deliverance

Made in the USA
Middletown, DE
14 April 2024

52914070R00064